baby LLAMAS

KIM THOMPSON

CREATIVE EDUCATION • CREATIVE PAPERBACKS

CONT

ENTS

I AM A CRIA.

I am a baby llama.

I can be white, gray, brown, or black.
ear
eye
lips

My mom had just one baby.
She hums to me. I drink her milk.

I live in a herd. We are domesticated animals.

I live in the mountains. Thick hair keeps me warm. I look for plants to eat. I can live for many days without water.

My hooves
help me
climb.

When I am grown, I will carry heavy loads for people. My hair will be used to make warm clothes and blankets.

If I do not want to move, I spit and kick!

SPEAK AND LISTEN

Can you speak like a cria?

Baby llamas call and cry.

Listen to these sounds:

https://www.youtube.com/watch?v=Bt6sbT0d6S0

CRIA WORDS

domesticated: not wild; used to living with people

herd: a group of llamas that live and feed together

hooves: hard, nail-like coverings on a llama's feet

mountains: tall landforms that are higher than hills

READING CORNER

Bodden, Valerie. *Llamas (Amazing Animals)*. Mankato, Minn.: Creative Paperbacks, 2019.

Kellett, Jenny. *Llamas and Alpacas: The Ultimate Llama and Alpaca Book*. Melbourne, Australia: Bellanova Books, 2023.

Myers, Maya. *National Geographic Readers: Llamas*. Washington, D.C.: National Geographic Kids, 2020.

INDEX

PUBLISHED BY CREATIVE EDUCATION AND CREATIVE PAPERBACKS
P.O. Box 227, Mankato, Minnesota 56002
Creative Education and Creative Paperbacks are imprints of The Creative Company
www.thecreativecompany.us

LIBRARY OF CONGRESS CATALOGING-IN-PUBLICATION DATA
Names: Thompson, Kim, 1970- author.
Title: Baby llamas / Kim Thompson.
Description: Mankato, Minnesota : Creative Education and Creative Paperbacks, [2026] | Series: Starting out | Includes bibliographical references and index. | Audience: Ages 4-7 | Audience: Grades K-1 |
Summary: "Introduce beginning readers to the world of baby llamas with this life science starter. Includes photos, a labeled animal diagram, "Make a Noise" section, glossary, and further resources"-- Provided by publisher.
Identifiers: LCCN 2024043247 (print) | LCCN 2024043248 (ebook) | ISBN 9798889897491 (library binding) | ISBN 9781682778357 (paperback) | ISBN 9798889897620 (ebook)
Subjects: LCSH: Llamas--Infancy--Juvenile literature.
Classification: LCC SF401.L6 T46 2026 (print) | LCC SF401.L6 (ebook) | DDC 636.2/966--dc23/eng/20241228
LC record available at https://lccn.loc.gov/2024043247
LC ebook record available at https://lccn.loc.gov/2024043248

DESIGN AND PRODUCTION
Design by Rhea Magaro
Production by Beeline Media and Design, Inc.
Art direction by Tom Morgan

PHOTOGRAPHS by Alamy Stock Photo/imageBROKER.com GmbH & Co. KG, 11; Dreamstime/Belizar, 5, Piccaya, 12; Getty Images/ODD ANDERSEN, 2-3, wanderluster, 10-11, Wong Yu Liang, 14, Yann Guichaoua-Photos, 9; Shutterstock/a_v_d, 4, Bohbeh, 13, Geoff Hardy, 7, Peruphotart, 6-7, schusterbauer.com, cover, SERSOLL, 8

Printed in India